Stockholm combines a
ty with a vibrant city life
city's lake, forests and b
subway stations. Creativ
the countless museums, _____, shops and nightclubs
and see for yourself. The city is known for being in the forefront of
fashion, music and design. Keep an eye on Stockholm, as it continu-
ally influences and molds the artistic and cultural zeitgeist.

CITIx60: Stockholm explores the stunning Swedish capital in five as-
pects, covering architecture, art spaces, shops and markets, eating
and entertainment. With expert advice from 60 stars of the city's
creative scene, this book guides you to the real attractions of the
city for an authentic taste of Stockholm life.

Contents

Before You Go

BASIC INFO

Currency
Swedish Krona (SEK/kr)
Exchange rate: US$1 : 8.3 SEK

Time zone
GMT +1
DST +2

DST begins at 0200 (local time) on the last Sunday of March and ends at 0300 (local time) on the last Sunday of October.

Dialling
International calling: +46
Citywide (0)8*

* Add (0) for calls made within Sweden.

Weather (avg. temperature range)
Spring (Mar-May): -3-16°C / 27-61°F
Summer (June-Aug): 10-21°C / 50-70°F
Autumn (Sep-Nov): 1-14°C / 34-57°F
Winter (Dec-Feb): -4-1°C / 25-34°F

USEFUL WEBSITES

Public transport info & travel planner
sl.se/en

Tax free shopping guide & refund calculator (purchases above 200 SEK)
www.globalblue.com/destinations/sweden

Festivals & shows ticketing
www.ticnet.se

EMERGENCY CALLS

Ambulance, fire or police
122

Embassies
France	+46 (0)8 459 53 00
Germany	+46 (0)8 670 15 00
Japan	+46 (0)8 579 353 00
Spain	+46 (0)8 522 808 00
UK	+46 (0)8 671 30 00
US	+46 (0)8 783 53 00

AIRPORT EXPRESS TRANSFER

Arlanda Airport <-> Stockholm Central Station (Arlanda Express)
Trains / Journey: every 15 mins / 20 mins
From Arlanda Airport – 0505-0105
From Stockholm Central Station (platforms 1 & 2) – 0435-0035
One-way: 280 SEK / Return: 530 SEK
www.arlandaexpress.com

Skavsta Airport <-> Stockhlom City Terminal (Flygbussarna Airport Coaches)
Bus / Journey: every 20-60 mins / 80 mins
From Skavsta Airport – 0730-2355 (M,W), 0000-(Tu, Th-Su)*
From Stockholm City Terminal – 0330-1900*
One-way: 159 SEK / Return: 285 SEK
www.flygbussarna.se/en

* Departure times may vary on specific dates. Please check online.

PUBLIC TRANSPORT IN STOCKHOLM

Metro
Light Rail
Commuter train
Bus
Tram
Ferry

Means of Payment
Credit card
Cash

PUBLIC HOLIDAYS

January	1 New Year's Day, 6 Epiphany
Mar/Apr	Good Friday, Easter Monday
May	1 May Day, Ascension Day
June	6 National Day, Midsummer's Eve & Day
Oct/Nov	All Saints' Day
December	24 Christmas Eve, 25 Christmas Day, 26 Boxing Day, 31 New Year's Eve

*Museums and galleries are likely to take summer breaks between June and August.

FESTIVALS / EVENTS

April
Kulturnatt Stockholm
kulturnattstockholm.se

June
Summerburst Festival
summerburst.se/stockholm

July
Stockholm Pride (through to August)
www.stockholmpride.org
Stockholm Street Festival
stockholmstreetfestival.com

August
Popaganda
www.popaganda.se
Midnattsloppet
www.midnattsloppet.com
Stockholm Music & Arts Festival
stockholmmusicandarts.com
Stockholms Kulturfestival
kulturfestivalen.stockholm.se

September
Stockholm Beer & Whiskey Festival
(Through to October)
www.stockholmbeer.se

October
Stockholm Jazz Festival
www.stockholmbeer.se

November
Stockholm International Film Festival
www.stockholmfilmfestival.se

December
Nobel Day
www.nobelprize.org

Event days vary by year. Please check for
updates online.

UNUSUAL OUTINGS

The Green Trails
www.thegreentrails.com

Stockholm Ghost Walk
www.stockholmghostwalk.com

Rooftop Tours
www.takvandring.com/en/home

Swedish Tramway Society
www.djurgardslinjen.se

Millennium Tour
www.stadsmuseet.stockholm.se/In-English/
Guided-tours/Millennium/

ABBA City Walk
www.stadsmuseet.stockholm.se/In-English/
Guided-tours/ABBA-City-Walk

SMARTPHONE APP

Public transport ticketing & travel planner
SL-biljetter

Archipelago ferries ticket info & timetables
Waxholmsbolaget

WiFi hotspots locator
WiFi Map

Learning to speak daily Swedish
Swedish by Nemo

REGULAR EXPENSES

A double espresso
25 SEK

Domestic / International mail (postcards)
6 SEK/12 SEK

Gratuities
At restaurants & bars: Round up to the
nearest SEK
On licensed taxis: 5 to 10% of payment

Count to 10

What makes Stockholm so special?

Illustrations by Guillaume Kashima aka Funny Fun

Stockholm is well-known for being in the forefront of fashion, music and design. Think: minimalistic fashion, electronic pop music, clean lines and sustainable design. Nature holds the hand of the city. Young-sters dive into Lake Mälaren for a midnight dip, just a few steps away from Central Station. Whether you are on a one-day stopover or a week-long stay, see what Stockholm creatives consider essential to see, taste, visit and take home from your trip.

1

Architecture

5

Classic Food

Tunnbrödsrulle with shrimp salad
Any hotdog stand

Herring & snaps
Sturehof, www.sturehof.com

Meatballs
Tranan, www.tranan.se
Pelikan (#40)

Kräftor (crayfish)
Urban Deli, www.urbandeli.org

Fried Baltic herring
Strömmingsvagnen (Herring
truck), Södermalmstorg, 116 45

Kanelbulle (cinnamon rolls)
Tössebageriet, FB: Tössebageriet
Rosendals Tradgard,
www.rosendalstradgard.se

6

Fika Spots

Drop Coffee
Coffee roastery with a coffee bar
www.dropcoffee.com

Spånga Konditori
Coffee & cakes
www.spangakonditori.se

18 smaker
Homemade ice-cream
www.18smaker.se

Chutney
Vegetarian food & vegan pastries
chutney.se

Johan & Nyströms
Weekly coffee choices
johanochnystrom.se

Kafé 44
vegan food, coffee & show nights
kafe44.org

Valand Kafé Konditori (#44)

7

Locally Made Products

Dalahäst (Wooden Dala Horse)
Wooden Horse Museum
woodenhorsemuseumsweden.se

Bikes & accessories
BIKEID
bikeid.se

Toffees & caramel candies
Pärlans Konfektyr
www.parlanskonfektyr.se

Handmade glass & ceramic
blås & knåda
www.blasknada.com

Perfume, body care & fragrances
Byredo Parfume
byredo.com

Specialty craft beer
Omnipollo, Omnipollos Hatt (#58)
www.omnipollo.com

Mohawk beer
mohawkbrewing.se

8

Seasonal Activities

Celebrate Midsummer
sweden.se/culture-traditions/
midsummer

**Summerbio (Summer cinema)
@Rålambshovsparken**
www.stockholmfilmfestival.se

Picnic on the rocks of Fredhäll
Bring a one-off BBQ and throw
on a couple of *korv med bröd*
(sausages with bread)

**Eat Semla (almond
paste-stuffed bun in hot cream)**
Every Tuesday between Shrove
Tuesday and Easter
Linquists Konditori, *www.
lindquists.nu*

Ice plunge & sauna in winter
Hellasgården
www.hellasgarden.se/en

Skating on frozen lakes
in Stockholm archipelago (#12)

9

Leisurely Routes

View graffiti on Pendeltåg
between Spånga & Karlberg stations
sl.se/en

**A nice view of Gamla Stan (#6)
& the city hall (#7)**
Monteliusvägen walkway

Self-guided city tour on a bike
Årstabroarna (the Årsta bridges),
Västerbron (The Western
Bridge); Norr Mälarstrand, Söder
Mälarstrand (Northern Shore of
Mälaren); around Årstaviken; or in
Skeppsholmen

Dinner cruise to Vaxholm
www.blidosundsbolaget.se/en/
dinner-cruises/

A walk on a waterfront boulevard
Strandvägen, Östermalm

10

Homegrown Labels

Backpacks, tote bags, wallets
Sandqvist
www.sandqvist.net

Fashionable ready-to-wear
Acne Studios, acnestudios.com
Filippa K, www.filippa-k.com

Sneakers
Eytys
www.eytys.com

Sustainable looks for men
Uniforms for the Dedicated
uniformsforthededicated.com

Statement jewellery
j0o0lry, j0o0lry.com

Clean fashion & denim designs
Weekday
www.weekday.com

Women's fashion
Monki
www.monki.com

Icon Index

 Opening hours

 Address

 Contact

Remarks

 Admission

 Facebook

 Website

 Scan QR codes to access Google Maps and discover the area around each destination. Internet connection required.

60x60

60 Local Creatives x 60 Hotspots

From vast cityscapes to the tiniest glimpses of everyday exchange, there is much to provoke one's imagination. 60x60 points you to 60 haunts where 60 arbiters of taste develop their good taste.

Landmarks & Architecture   SPOTS · 01 – 12

Nature is in the heart of Stockholm's city life. Take a ferry and discover the rustic Swedish archipelago. Explore Modernist and Nordic Classical buildings from the likes of Gunnar Asplund.

Cultural & Art Spaces   SPOTS · 13 – 24

Take in modern art and photography, and relish in classical Scandinavian paintings in the many vibrant museums and galleries. Stockholm is in the forefront of music, design and arts.

Markets & Shops   SPOTS · 25 – 36

Stockholm is a treasure trove of vintage stores, minimalist fashion and design shops. Retro accessories, stunning textiles and quirky handmade comic books — take your pick.

Restaurants & Cafés   SPOTS · 37 – 48

This city is a delightful playground for coffee and cake lovers. Enjoy lavish Swedish cuisine, or try out something more cosmopolitan. Don't leave town without eating a *kannelbulle*.

Nightlife   SPOTS · 49 – 60

Catch a concert at a lively venue, have drinks while watching the sunset and dance under a bridge. Beer is expensive but it won't stop you from having a fantastic night out in town.

Landmarks & Architecture

Nordic Classicism, a charming Old Town and idyllic islands

Straddling Lake Mälaren and the Baltic Sea, Stockholm's unique landscape is a sight to behold. Wide avenues and tall, yellow ochre 19th-century buildings, combined with shimmering bodies of water and sporadic forests give the feeling of vastness and tranquility. You are never truly far from nature in this city, as seen in the works of Swedish architects such as Gunnar Asplund's (1885–1940) creations. Surrounded by trees and sloping fields, his stunning woodland cemetery Skogskyrkogården (#9), combines modern architecture in the Nordic Classicist style with equally beautiful natural surroundings. It is a perfect place for an introspective morning walk and quiet reflection. In the afternoon, explore the cobbled stone streets of Gamla Stan (#6), get a glimpse of its famed medieval architecture and a taste of local history and pause for a *fika* at one of the many cosy cellar cafés nearby. During the warmer months, pack a picnic basket and take a stroll up the rocky cliffs of Skinnarviksberget (#11), Stockholm's highest natural point, for a spectacular view of the city's skyline and a welcome breeze. A trip to Stockholm is not complete without an excursion to the beautiful islands of the Stockholm Archipelago (#12). Ideas Island in Vifärnaholme offers a free week's stay in an idyllic location, for creatives to work on their projects; while Värmdö island houses the stunning Artipelag (#15) – a must for both architecture and nature lovers. The scenic boat trip to the islands is already an experience in itself.

Filmhuset
P.016

Martin Falck
Graphic designer

I'm a graphic designer and visual researcher working with print design, music, art direction, video, fashion and animation.

Anders Kornestedt
Partner, Happy F&B

Happy F&B's mission is to nurture and release great ideas. By marrying a far-sighted strategy with design, we help develop brands that make a world of real difference.

Ramiro Oblitas
Cofounder, Parasol

I am a quadrilingual graphic design and branding specialist with 15+ years of international experience working across sectors including aviation, public transport and retail.

Stockholms
Tunnelbana
P.014

Sven-Harrys
Konst-
museum
P.017

Daniel Mair
Creative consultant & designer

I run my own multidisciplinary studio Mair / Wennel and teach at Konstfack in Stockholm. After living in London for ten years, I see and appreciate Stockholm in a different way.

Stockholms
Stads-
bibliotek
P.019

Virpi Pahkinen
Choreographer & dancer

Born in Finland, I've performed on the big stages and steppes in over 45 countries. I'm a master of traveling with light luggage, and believer of discipline with a lust for improvisation.

FORM US WITH LOVE
Design studio

For the last decade, we've put dialogue and relevance at its core, using clever design to position, build and sustain brands of tomorrow. Past collaborators include Ikea, Muuto and Absolut.

Ericsson
Globe
P.018

Gamla Stan
P.020

Clara von Zweigbergk
Art director & product designer

I was born in Stockholm and work as a graphic designer currently in pursuit of my great interest in paper, color, typography and form.

David Ericsson
DAVID ERICSSON Design Studio

For me "zeitgeist" is important because we are living in a time of change. Besides DAVID ERICSSON, I also co-founded DMOCH and teach at Carl Malmsten Furniture Studies.

Petter Johansson
Creative director & CEO, PJADAD

PJADAD works across disciplines independent of media. Recent works include IKEA's design collection "IKEA PS 2012" with a global multi-channel campaign.

Herr Nilsson
Street artist

I'm a visual activist based in Stockholm. I'm most known for my Dark Princess series, violent Winnie the Pooh and Hello Kitty paintings.

Anna Lidberg
Founder, Gallery 1:10

Besides curation, I create video installations, objects and social projects, often exploring issues of art's accessibility, power structures and their relationship with the spectator.

Oskar Lübeck
Founder, Bold

I'm the founder and executive creative director of design agency Bold. After some years abroad I now spend most of my time on Södermalm, where I live with my wife and two kids.

1 Stockholms Tunnelbana

Engulfed in mosaics, paintings, installations and engravings, Stockholm's subway stations have been an astounding spectacle since the 1950s. The first metro stations were built during a time of socialist influence over politics and the dream and belief in the welfare state. More than 150 artists have left their voice in over 90 stations out of 100, turning public art into a historical monument. If you don't have time for station-hopping, be sure you at least stop by the harlequin Kungsträdgården on the blue line, and Östermalmstorg on the red where Siri Derkert saluted women's rights, world peace and the green movement.

🕐 Opening hours vary by station   🔗 sl.se/en
📎 Free EN guided tour: 1500 (Tu, Th, Sa, Jun 2–
Aug 29), sl.se/en/eng-info/contact/art-walks

"The trip from the inner city to the outer suburbs is amazing. There is a guided tour but my advice would be to just travel by yourself and really go everywhere."

– Martin Falck

2 Filmhuset
Map H, P.109

Conceived by Peter Celsing (1920–74), the
Swedish Film Institute building completed in
1970 is typical for the architect's brutalist style.
The abundance of grey concrete surfaces,
filmstrip-inspired window lines, film reels-like
stairwells were all Celsing's riposte to the
Institute's founder's request for a "no ordinary
bloody building" to promote film making and
appreciation. Architecture buffs should also
stroll the Gärdet area to contemplate more
great buildings from the era, like the Kaknäs
Tower at Mörka Kroken 28–30, and Garnisonen,
an expansive office complex at Karlavägen 100.

🕐 0800–2000 (Tu–Su), –1800 (M), Jun 20–mid-Aug:
0800–1800 (M–F) 🏠 Borgvägen 1–5, 115 53
🔗 www.sfi.se/filmhuset

"This is one of Peter Celsing's public buildings that
present radical modernism with a lot of intellectual
layers."

– Anders Kornestedt, Happy F&B

3 Sven-Harrys Konstmuseum
Map A, P.104

Instead of donating to another museum, art collector Sven-Harry Karlsson made his own next to Vasaparken. Designed by Wingårdhs Architects, this wonderfully golden brass-clad building attracts the public to view Karlsson's Nordic art collections at his "home", above 400 square-metres of active living spaces and bright galleries where multifaceted exhibitions primarily of Swedish contemporary artists rotate. All visits to the home are by guided tours only. The terrace is open to visitors when the weather permits.

🕐 1100–1900 (W–Fr), –1700 (Sa–Su)
💲 150/130 SEK (incl. Sven-Harry's home)
🏠 Eastmansvägen 10–12, 113 61
📞 +46 (0)8 511 600 60 URL www.sven-harrys.se
📎 Advanced booking required for non-Swedish private guided tours

"The exterior is cladded in a metal called Nordic Royal, the yellow facade is truly fantastic."

– Ramiro Oblitas, Parasol

4 Ericsson Globe
Map C, P.105

As well as a concert arena, Ericsson Globe also represents "the Sun" in the Sweden Solar System, the world's largest model of the Solar System that spans the entire country. It began as academics Nils Brenning and Gösta Gahm saw the largest hemispherical building built in 1989. The system has been growing since, with artists interpreting the "planets", accurately resized and spaced out on the scale of 1:20 million. While the furthermost celestial body is yet to be realised in Kiruna, feel the sense of scale as you view "Mercury" as a 25cm metallic sphere at the Stockholm City Museum. The ball is heated to symbolise its proximity to the Sun.

🏠 Globentorget 2, 121 27
URL swedensolarsystem.se 📎 Stockholm City Museum is closed till autumn 2017.

"Visit the Sweden Solar System site and use it as a guide. The Globe looks best from Södermalm, no point in going up close."
– Daniel Mair

5 Stockholms Stadsbibliotek
Map A, P.104

Designed by Gunnar Asplund (1885–1940) and opened in 1928, Stockholm City Library was the first in the country to offer public access to the stacks, applying America's practice. Comprised of reading rooms in the cubic plinth and a lending hall with tiered bookshelves in the rotunda, the geometric structure is considered a stark Nordic Classicist composition. Tailored furniture, the children's storytelling room and the drinking fountains in the reading rooms are of special note. Caruso St John behind Tate Britain art gallery's renovation will be helming the library's restructuring from 2017 to 2019.

🕙 0900-2100 (M-Th), -1900 (F), 1200-1600(Sa-Su)
🏠 Sveavägen 73, 113 80 ☎ +46 (0)8 508 309 00
URL biblioteket.stockholm.se

"Try and hide in the poetry corner and read one book you never planned to read."
– Virpi Pahkinen

6 Gamla Stan

Map D, P.106

Skip the touristy Västerlånggatan and wander the narrow streets of Old Town where Stockholm was found in 1252. Medieval alleyways, cobblestone streets and archaic architecture give this area its unique identity, among nice little shops, eating places and bars where you can even specifically book a Chesterfield armchair for a comfy night, or live jazz plays almost every night. Reserve time for such landmarks as Stockholm Cathedral, the Nobel Museum and Riddarholmen Church, a former monastery on the adjacent island of Riddarholmen. Complete you trip with some authentic Nordic home cooking at Den Gyldene Freden.

URL *Den Gyldene Freden: gyldenefreden.se
Stampen: www.stampen.se,
Tweed: www.tweed.se*

"Eat at Den Gyllene Freden to fully experience the old vibe."

– FORM US WITH LOVE

7. Stadshuset

Map F, P.108

An iconic National Romantic masterpiece, the seminal Stockholm City Hall stands over Stockholm's cityscape. It houses the city's Municipal Council and carries the Swedish royal crowns, 106 metres up in the air above its lantern-topped spire. Guided tours offer the only chance for the public to view its ceremonial halls, notably the mosaiced Golden Hall and the Blue hall, where the annual Nobel Prize banquet takes place. Visits to the tower and the museum are organised at 40 minutes intervals and limited to 30 visitors a time.

🕐 By guided tour only: 1000-1500 daily (EN), Tower: 0915-1715 (Jun-Aug), -1555 (May & Sep) 💲 100/80/40 SEK (Apr-Oct), 70/60/20 SEK (Nov-Mar), Tower: 50 SEK 🏠 Hantverkargatan 1, 111 52 📞 +46 (0)8 508 290 58 URL international. stockholm.se/the-city-hall 🔗 All tours are subject to change. No booking required.

"The garden stairs lead right into the water, perfect for a swim!"

– Clara von Zweigbergk

8 Markuskyrkan
Map M, P.110

Set in a thinly planted birch grove separate from the nondescript suburb apartments in Björkhagen, this beautiful 1960 brickwork speaks with architect Sigurd Lewerentz's (1885–1975) posit to establish symbolism through materiality, craftsmanship and the use of light. This comes clear as one progresses from daylight to darkness by rambling through multiple recesses and entering the nave. Architectural details, decorative works and bespoke light fittings and pews slowly reveal as one adapts to the pitch dark room. Visit on a Sunday by 10.30am to hear the church bells ring.

🕐 0830–1630 (M, W–F), –1830 (Tu), 0900–1500 (Sa–Su)
🏠 Malmövägen 51, 121 53   ☎ +46 (0)8 505 815 00
🔗 www.svenskakyrkan.se/skarpnack/
markuskyrkan (SE)

"After visiting the church you can walk about 25 minutes and see the UNESCO World Heritage Skogskyrkogården (#9)."

– David Ericsson, DAVID ERICSSON Design Studio

9 Skogskyrkogården
Map O, P.110

Stretching out on a vast park area, the Woodland Cemetery stands for a new memorial garden concept in the early 1900s, credited to architects Gunnar Asplund and Sigurd Lewerentz. Beautiful pavilions, pine forest and artistic decoration blend into a harmonic whole, including a giant granite cross that symbolises the cycle of life and death in the multi-ethnic burial ground. All chapels and crematoriums, including the red-brick addition by Johan Celsing, can only be visited by guided tours. A public bus service leaves every 30 minutes from outside the Skogskyrkogården station with several stops inside the cemetery.

🏠 Sockenvägen, 122 33
🔗 www.skogskyrkogarden.stockholm.se
🔗 EN guided tours: 1030 (Su, Jul–Sep), 100 SEK.
Advanced booking recommended.

"Consider this the only real interesting art space here."

– Petter Johansson, PJADAD

10 Tranebergsbron
Map L, P.110

Spanning a length of 450 metres, the 1934 Traneberg Bridge built by modernist architect Paul Hedqvist (1895–1977) once boasted the world's largest concrete vault. A road and pedestrian sidewalk are situated on the bridge for crossing the strait Tranebergssund, commanding a stunning panorama of the central part of Stockholm. The underside of the bridge is also worth checking out for its gigantic pillars, where street art is repeatedly created and quickly cleaned. Take the subway to Alvik station and follow Tranebergsvägen to a dirt road that leads to the foundation of the bridge. Painters be warned: the bridge is under the Commuter Security guard's watch.

🏠 *Alvik, Kristineberg*

"*The urban sounds of traffic 30 metres up, the beautiful view of the city and the waterfront make this my favourite place in Stockholm.*"

– Herr Nilsson

11 Skinnarviksberget
Map I, P.109

At a height of 50 some metres, Skinnarviks-berget is Stockholm's highest natural point where you can escape the urban grind and just gaze at central parts of Stockholm. The rocky viewing point and park with an Arne Jones sculpture is quite popular for summer barbeques, picnics or sunset views, particularly during the warmer months of the year. Nearby Ivar Los Park at Blecktornsgränd 1 also offers breathtaking views of the city, with traces of Söder's working class history. Take Tavastgatan and you'll pass by Teenage Engineering's showroom at no. 15.

🏠 Söder Mälarstrand, 118 23

"If you wish to bring your own alcoholic drinks, the best place to get them is Systembolaget. It closes in the evening and most of the weekends. So plan ahead."

– Anna Lidberg, Gallery 1:10

12 Stockholms Skärgård

A tourist destination in its own right, no trip to Stockholm is complete without exploring the rugged natural beauty of the archipelago. With its 30,000 small islands of picturesque, largely untouched wooded islands, rocky cliffs and sandy beaches, it is a unique and truly inspiring place that brings out your inner explorer. Outdoor pursuits like fishing, hiking, cycling, camping and swimming are popular, as are the many cultural districts which offer some of the finest hotels in the city. Check website for unique excursions or "Count to 10" for highlights.

URL *stockholmarchipelago.se*

"Torö is my all-time favourite. My wife and I fell so hard for the island that we bought a vacation house there. It's known for its waves, and Stenstrand has the best."

– Oskar Lübeck, Bold

029

Cultural & Art Spaces

Trendsetting art, splendid photography and melancholic classics

Stockholm takes the lead in international arts and design industries, a city where creativity is seen and felt almost everywhere, and where its residents are early adopters of upcoming global trends. Sustainability, innovation and openness are values that resonate with Swedish thinking, ideas and creative pursuits. Take a peek at Stockholm's most edgy art collection at Magasin III (#18), bask in glorious modern photography at the beautiful Fotografiska (#17) and keep up with the latest contemporary art, fashion and design trends at Liljevalchs (#21). If it's natural beauty that captures your imagination, take a boat trip to Artipelag (#15), located in the Swedish archipelago. The vast modern architecture combined with the rugged beauty of the surrounding lake and forest, is breathtaking. Modern art lovers should also visit Moderna Museet (#16), and neighbouring ArkDes for a slice of architectural history. In addition to the two, Djurgården island is filled to the brim with excellent (and more classical) museums including Vasamuseet, Prins Eugens Waldemarsudde and Thielska Galleriet. The moody late 19th and early 20th century painting collections of the latter two capture the essence of the Swedish soul. Speaking of impressive paintings, don't miss out on Biologiska Museet's (#20) captivating 360-degree bird diorama painted by renowned Swedish painter Bruno Liljefors (1860–1939). To round up your art-filled day, check out the performance listings at Färgfabriken (#14), housed in a former colour-making factory, for experimental art exhibitions, concerts and regular flea markets.

Jenny Theolin
Owner, Studio Theolin

I'm an active writer, creative director, curator and producer heading up StudioTheolin that specialises in visual arts, music and culture. I also run a MA programme at Hyper Island.

Kulturhuset Stadsteatern
P.034

Färgfabriken
P.035

Johanna Irander
Founder, Studio Irander

I set up Studio Irander in The Hague in 2007. The office is currently based in Stockholm, working within the fields of landscape architecture and urban planning.

Fredrik Wikholm
Uniforms for the Dedicated

I cofounded and creatively direct both the label and initiative, The Ragbag. Sustainability, music, people and challenges are dear to me. Stockholm is great but even greater coming back to.

Artipelag
P.036

Stockholm Design Lab
Branding agency

SDL transforms brands and businesses with simple, remarkable ideas. We keep an unswerving focus on what lasts. On truth, not triviality. And on intelligence, not speculation.

Moderna Museet
P.038

Fotografiska
P.039

Sara N Bergman
Illustrator

I'm a children's book illustrator, and stylist and designer of Love Warriors. I was born in southern Sweden and moved here in the 1990s. Love every part of my job and my hometown.

Fredric Benesch & Katarina Lundeberg

We are architects, critics and the founders of In Praise of Shadows Arkitektur, engaged in several housing projects and Aesop stores. We also teaches at the KTH Architecture School.

Magasin III
P.040

Emma Löfström
Artist

I am an image-maker, working with drawings and collage whilst exploring multilayered human conditions. I've partaken in The White Building's Iaspis residency programme in 2015.

Biologiska Museet
P.042

Mathias Sterner
Photographer & director

I have a sore spot for mother nature's grand spectacles and spend a lot of time on Öland where I'm originally from. My most recent fascination is plants. To grow stuff is pretty awesome!

Jens Assur
Photographer & filmmaker

I work as a still photographer and filmmaker driven by an inexhaustible curiosity about our contemporary world. Through my work, I spur people on to reflect about how we live our lives.

Marabou-parken
P.041

Liljevalchs
P.044

Lisa Ullenius & Sissi Edholm, *Edholm Ullenius*

We are a graphic design and illustration studio which sees the result of every project a pure dialogue with lust and surprise. Since 2002, we've clients ranging from Ikea and Paul Smith.

Kultur-föreningen Tellus
P.046

Marcus Lindeen
Writer & director

I write and direct films and theater plays. My work is mostly based on documentary materials, so I spend a lot of time on research and interviews. I am about to move to Midsommarkransen.

Veronica Wallenberg
Director, Cinematic

I am a director at animation studio Cinematic. I'm a huge travel enthusiast and will spend big parts of the year travelling albeit mostly working at the same time.

Hallwylska Museet
P.045

Seriegalleriet
P.047

13 Kulturhuset Stadsteatern
Map F, P.108

Architect Peter Celsing's vision to create an accessible 'culture lounge' was finally realised as Kulturhuset opened in 1974. Often compared to the Centre Pompidou in Paris, the complex building encourages visitors to navigate the space over several floors. Alongside an ambitious programme of modern theatre, art exhibitions, performance and literature events, Kulturhuset also runs interesting smaller scale activities. Parkteatern is one such highlight, welcoming visitors of all ages to enjoy performance theatre in a less formal, outdoor setting.

🕐 1100–1900 (M–F), –1700 (Sa–Su)
🏠 Sergels torg, 103 27 📞 +46 (0)8 506 202 00
URL kulturhusetstadsteatern.se

"Take time to visit its wonderful roof-top terrace. It's perfect for an arty meander, a read in the library, or a G&T in the sun."

– Jenny Theolin, Studio Theolin

16 Moderna Museet
Map D, P.106

Beautifully situated on Skeppsholmen island, the Museum of Modern Art houses Swedish and international modern and contemporary art as well as one of the largest Nordic specialised libraries for art, photography and design. Gaze at Swedish painter Nils Dardel's post-impressionist gem The Dying Dandy (1918) and marvel at its intensity of colours and emotions, alongside key pieces by Duchamp, Magritte and a model of the Tatlin's Tower. With reduced admission, you can combine your visit with ArkDes, the Swedish Centre for Architecture and Design, next door.

🕐 1000–2000 (Tu, F), –1800 (W–Th, Sa–Su)
💲 120/100 SEK 🏠 Slupskjulsvägen 7, 111 49
📞 +46 (0)8 520 235 00
🔗 www.modernamuseet.se 📎 Museum takes summer break, normally from mid June to August.

"The museum was first opened in 1958 and in 2004 Stockholm Design Lab designed its current visual identity."

– Stockholm Design Lab

 Fotografiska
Map E, P.107

Presenting four major exhibitions annually, alongside a number of minor exhibitions, Fotografiska is the only institution in Stockholm that focuses purely on photography. Past events include a retrospective of American portrait photographer Annie Leibovitz, and a curated exhibition of polaroid portraits by acclaimed filmmaker Gus Van Sant. The museum also boasts a renowned restaurant which is an experience in itself, where flavours, scents, materials and environment are all part of a carefully prepared package. Diners can bask in the spectacular view over the lake and enjoy occasional live music in the summer.

🕐 0900–2300 daily 💲 120/90 SEK
🏠 Stadsgårdshamnen 22, 116 45
📞 +46 (0)8 520 235 00
🔗 fotografiska.eu
📎 Museum closes on Midsummer's Eve and Christmas Eve. 45-min guided tour: 600–1200 SEK/25pax, booking required

"Shop in the day and visit the museum at night since it opens till late. The view from the restaurant is stunning. Book ahead if you want a table indoor!"

– Sara N Bergman

18 Magasin III
Map H, P.109

Lodged into an old warehouse on a former freeport, Magasin III runs as a private institution and is home to Stockholm's most edgy modern art collection, featuring everything from art by Ai WeiWei to dreamy video installations by Pipilotti Rist. As well as a foundation for contemporary art, the museum hosts a diverse programme of exhibitions and a two-year Master programme in Art Curation with Stockholm University since 2003. Equally good are their café and reference library full of exhibition catalogues and artist's books.

🕐 1100–1900 (Th), –1700 (F–Su) except between exhibitions 💲 80/60 SEK 🏠 1st Fl., Frihamnen, Frihamnsgatan 28, 115 56 📞 +46 (0)8 545 680 40 🔗 www.magasin3.com 🖉 Summer break runs from June to mid September. Group tour: 1,500 SEK/30pax, booking required

"Go there and look into their drawing collection, their fantastic library of art books and the very nice café, out in the harbour area."

– Fredric Benesch & Katarina Lundeberg, In Praise of Shadows Arkitektur

19 Marabouparken
Map J, P.110

What used to be Marabou's cocoa laboratory and chocolate factory is now a lively meeting place for contemporary art. Built in the 1950s, Marabouparken art gallery regularly engages artists and visitors to reflect and explore issues in today's society with themed workshops, forums and film programmes, alongside artist collaborations scattered throughout the Arthur von Schmalensee architecture. Every year, the gallery participates in Stockholm Art Week, celebrating the local art scene through a packed programme of art fairs, exhibitions and events.

🕐 1200–2000 (W), –1700 (Tu–Su)
💲 50 SEK
🏠 Löfströmsvägen 8, 172 66
📞 +46 (0)8 294 590
🔗 marabouparken.se

"Attached to the gallery is a beautiful sculpture park initially installed as a recreational facility for the factory workers in the 1950s."

– Emma Löfström

20 Biologiska Museet
Map B, P.105

Founded by taxidermist, amateur zoologist and author Gustaf Kolthoff, the Biological Museum opened in 1893, displaying a vast collection of Scandinavian mammals and birds in their natural environment. The highlight of the museum is its impressive and pioneering diorama featuring hand-painted backgrounds by renowned Swedish painter Bruno Liljefors (1860–1939). The architecture is just as stunning as well, as architect Agi Lundgren referenced medieval Norwegian stave churches' designs when he conceived the building.

🕐 Oct–Mar: 1200–1500 (Tu–F), 1100– (Sa–Su), Apr–Sep: 1100–1600 daily 💲 65/50/25 SEK
🏠 Hazeliusporten, 115 93 📞 +46 (0)8 442 8215
🔗 www.biologiskamuseet.com

"It's somewhat a weird yet amazing and beautiful place. You might wish to spend a few hours with the beautiful surroundings and other great museums on Djurgården."
– Mathias Sterner

21 Liljevalchs
Map B, P.105

Girdled by the beautiful natural surroundings of Djurgården, Liljevalchs art gallery was
established in 1916 as the first independent,
public museum for contemporary art in Sweden. Designed by Carl Bergsten, the Liljevalchs
presents at least four large exhibitions each
year showcasing contemporary art, fashion
and design trends, alongside their famous
juried Vårsalongen (Spring Salon). Don't forget
to check out the museum store, where you
can pick up quirky design souvenirs. Nearby
Prins Eugens Waldemarsudde and Thielska Galleriet are also worth taking a peek for classical
Scandinavian and Swedish paintings.

🕐 1100–2000 (Tu,Th), –1700 (W, F–Su)
💲 10 SEK 🏠 Djurgårdsvägen 60, 115 21
📞 +46 (0)8 508 313 30 🔗 www.liljevalchs.se

*"Visit Liljevalchs during its famous Spring Salon, where
non-professionals come to show their work to a grand
audience. Everything is for sale, at reasonable price."*
– Jens Assur

22 Hallwylska museet
Map D, P.106

Escape to a different time as you visit the grand former home of Count Walther and Countess Wilhelmina von Hallwyl. One of the most expensive private residences ever built Sweden, the home was completed 1898 and later on it turned into a museum. Hallwylska Museet houses the family's fantastic personal art, porcelain and jewellery collection dating from the early 20th century. Take a peek inside its preserved rooms from the late Victorian period in Sweden, and have a glimpse into the lavish lifestyles of the nobility in Stockholm at the time.

🕐 Oct–May: 1200–1600 (Tu–Su), –1900(W), Jun: 1000–1600 (Tu–Su), Jul–Aug: 1000–1600 (Tu & Su), –1900 (W–Sa) 💲 90 SEK 🏠 Hamngatan 4, 111 47
📞 +46 (0)8 402 3099 🔗 www.hallwylskamuseet.se
✏️ Guided tour: 120 SEK

"Step 100 years back in time!"
– Lisa Ullenius & Sissi Edholm, Edholm Ullenius

23 Kulturföreningen Tellus
Map N, P.110

Tellus is the true cultural heart of Midsommarkransen, an up-and-coming area in the
south of Stockholm. The theatre opened at
their current address Vattenledningsvägen 46
in 1920 and was run as a commercial movie
theatre until the mid-eighties, when it was
taken over by a non-profit organisation. Tellus
is one of the few independent cinemas left in
Stockholm, but it offers much more than just
film screenings. Events include after-work
jazz concerts, poetry readings, art exhibitions,
knitting clubs, game nights and language ex-
changes. They have pretty tasty cakes as well.

🕐 **S** *Showtime and ticket price vary with*
programmes 🏠 *Vattenledningsvägen 46, 126 33*
📞 *+46 (0)8 645 7551* 🔲 *www.tellusbio.nu*

"Go to Midsommarkransen and walk around
this neighbourhood. There's a little park called
Svandammsparken and a great café for 'smørrebrød'."
– Marcus Lindeen

24 Seriegalleriet
Map I, P.109

Seriegalleriet sells original artwork from well-known comic books, picture books and animated films. A haven for comic enthusiasts and illustration aficionados, the rolling programme of mini exhibitions attracts visitors in search of highly collectable, limited edition artworks. The gallery is located in the hip Södermalm area, between Slussen and Mariatorget subway stations. It is in close proximity to Rival Hotel and Bar, owned by ABBA star Benny Andersson, which is a great place to have a coffee break (or *fika* as Swedes call it) in between shopping.

🕐 1100–1800 (M–F), 1200–1600 (Sa), 1300– (Su)
🏠 Sankt Paulsgatan 14, 118 46
📞 +46 (0)8 702 2425   URL www.seriegalleriet.se

"*You can always visit (Staffars Serier at Bellmansgatan 26A) around the corner if you didn't get enough of this genre. They have lots of new and old comics.*"

– Veronica Wallenberg, Cinematic

Markets & Shops

Design lovers' heaven, Vintage Valhalla and quirky comics

Stockholm offers a wide array of boutiques and independent stores, with a spotlight on contemporary design and forward-thinking yet understated fashion. Take a whole day aside to do some shopping and exploring. The luxurious department store NK (*Hamngatan 18–20, 111 47*), housed in an impressive Art Nouveau building, offers Swedish designer clothing as well as furniture and home accessories from Design House Stockholm. Nearby Åhléns is a good place to stock up on affordable souvenirs, accessories, stationery and textiles. For minimalist fashion, check out Our Legacy (#26) for menswear, APLACE for the latest Scandinavian brands, and Acne Archive (*Torsgatan 53, 113 37*) for bargain steals on past collections. Grab a coffee, place yourself on Götgatan shopping street, where Swedish brands Weekday, Monki and Filippa K are also located, and watch stylish pedestrians walk by for a dose of inspiration. While Stockholm is known as a fashion and design-lover's shopping paradise, it is also a vintage heaven in terms of quality and quantity. Spend an afternoon visiting the city's best thrift stores for clothing bargains and one-of-a-kind accessories. Hunt the endless racks of clothing at Humana Second Hand (#33) for on-trend pieces at rock-bottom prices, as well as the popular Stockholm Stadsmission and Beyond Retro stores. For the ultimate collection of 1940s jewellery and vintage accessories, pop in at Antikt Gammalt & Nytt (#35). Love comics? Step into Papercut (#29), a popular spot for collectors and illustration fans. Take a short hop on the T-Bana, Stockholm's metro, also known as the world's longest art gallery (#1) to neighbouring Peow! (#30) to marvel at their collection of handmade comics and collectibles.

Lukas Rose
Strategic planner, House of Radon

German by origin, I've lived in Stockholm for five years and I truly love it. I spend my free time exploring concerts, museums, cafés and restaurants and like to share what I find.

Our Legacy
P.054

Thommy Bindefeld
Creative director, Svenskt Tenn

I'm responsible for the brand identity and securing the continuing long life of this historical interior company built on a philosophy of founder Estrid Ericson and architect Josef Frank.

Nick Ross
Founder, Nick Ross Design Studio

I run a design studio in the north of Stockholm. We work with furniture and lighting projects for commissions as well as research based studio projects.

Stutterheim
P.052

Svenskt Tenn
P.056

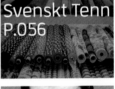

Henrik Franklin
Animator, cartoonist & curator

I'm a Konstfack graduate and one of the instigators of Book On the Fritz, a project that studies the morphology and development of publications through forums and exhibitions.

Papercut
P.059

Carl Kleiner
Photographer

I'm an image-maker, born, raised and based in Stockholm, most noted for my still-life photography created for Ikea, H&M, WALLPAPER* and AnOther Magazine.

Rui Tenreiro
Author, illustrator & art director

I create narrative experiences through storytelling, be it a book, film or piece of writing.

Rönnells
Antikvariat
P.058

Peow! Studio
P.060

Björn Atldax
Cofounder, Vår & Cheap Monday

I grew up in Siberia and am one half of design firm, Vår. I was responsible for Cheap Monday's brand style and artwork. Now I draw monsters, build sculptures of bones, freelance and cook.

Södermalms Akvarieaffär P.061

Brand– stationen P.062

Per Emanuelsson
Founder, Humans since 1982

I founded Humans since 1982 with Bastian Bischoff upon our graduation from Göteborgs universitet (HDK). Our work has appeared at museums, galleries and auctions worldwide.

Antikt Gammalt & Nytt P.066

Erik Bergqvist
Acne Advertising

I'm a creative director, father of one, owner of a dog and author of three books (all equally silly). I learnt my trade in London but moved back to Stockholm for the sake of love.

Viktor Khan
Animator & illustrator

I am an animator, graphic designer and illustrator residing in Stockholm. I animate dancing food items and hard working cats, and sometimes I do some serious work.

Humana Second Hand P.064

Tony Cederteg
Libraryman & Tony Cederteg

I'm founder of photo book pub–lisher Libraryman, design studio Tony Cederteg. Founder and creative director of film/fashion magazine Dogme. I travels often for work and to retain sanity.

Chez Albert P.067

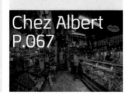

Linnea Olsson
Cellist, singer & composer

I've released two solo albums under my own name. I've lived in Stockholm for two years, so the city is pretty new to me. I'm slowly getting to know it.

Epok Antik & Kuriosa P.065

25 Stutterheim

Map E, P.107

Alexander Stutterheim launched his own brand of handmade raincoats as a homage to his late grandfather, whose old rain coat protected him on fishing trips out in Arholma (an island in the Stockholm archipelago). A wardrobe staple for many Stockholmers, this updated, contemporary version of the traditional raincoat is versatile and hard wearing, and is designed as a coat just as useful worn in the countryside, as strolling around the city. While in the area, grab a drink at the moody Vampire Lounge or enjoy a meal at the cosy Urban Deli.

🕐 1100–1800 (M–F), –1600 (Sa), 1200– (Su)
🏠 Åsögatan 132, 116 24
📞 +46 (0)8 408 103 98
URL www.stutterheim.com

"Twice a year, Stutterheim has a big sale of samples and last season's colours. It's usually mayhem, but if you're lucky, you can score a real bargain."

– Lukas Rose, House of Radon

26 Our Legacy
Map I, P.109

For the more fashion conscious traveller, a visit to Stockholm would not be complete without stepping inside Our Legacy. Known for its innovative yet understated menswear, the brand takes an inventive approach to fabric, infusing suiting, workwear and streetwear with distinct Scandinavian influences. Their artful minimalism has attracted a loyal following amongst Stockholm city dwellers and a few celebrity fans. If you feel the need to shop some more, right next door is Nitty Gritty, a popular store for designer clothing.

🕐 1100–1830 (M–F), –1700 (Sa), 1200–1600 (Su)
🏠 Jakobsbergsgatan 11, 111 44 📞 +46 (0)8 611 1010
URL www.ourlegacy.se
🖉 Check for closing days in summer

"Visit the store on Jakobsbergsgatan to see the beautiful interior by Arrhov Frick."

– Nick Ross

27 Svenskt Tenn
Map D, P.106

Historical and contemporary interior design meet at Svenskt Tenn. Founded in 1924 by designer and drawing teacher Estrid Ericson, Svenskt Tenn is known for its lush and stunning textile designs by Josef Frank, an Austrian-Jewish architect who developed his own type of modernism as a nod to the nature's wealth of colours and forms. Step into the store and be mesmerised with the elegant furniture, wallpapers, textiles and lighting, all produced by craftsmen in Sweden. Take advantage of Svenskt Tenn's expert service and take home a piece of classic Swedish design that is truly your type.

🕐 1000-1830 (M-F), -1700 (Tu), 1100-1600 (Sa) 🏠 Strandvägen 5, 114 51
📞 +46 (0)8 670 1600
🔗 www.svenskttenn.se

"Don't miss the tea room on the second floor."

– Thommy Bindefeld, Svenskt Tenn

28 Rönnells Antikvariat
Map A, P.105

One of Scandinavia's largest antiquarian book stores, Rönnells Antikvariat is a rare opportunity to explore beautiful things of the past. Opened in 1929, the store houses a 100,000-strong collection of books on every topic imaginable, from art to music, and from fiction to 19th century travel guides. Spend an afternoon foraging through the sales rack and take home a unique piece of history with you. The beautiful (and chic) Östermalm neighbourhood also has a lot to offer: watch a movie at Zita Folkets arthouse cinema, take a leisurely stroll at the romantic Humlegården park or grab a drink at Kåken.

🕙 1000–1800 (M–F), 1200–1600 (Sa–Su)
🏠 Birger Jarlsgatan 32, 114 29
📞 +46 (0)8 545 015 60
URL ronnells.se

"They have a wide variety of different genres including a really great art book section. The pop-up bookstores from guest curators are also a very nice touch."
– Henrik Franklin

29 Papercut
Map I, P.109

Papercut is a self-confessed 'magazine-junkie's paradise'. The shop stocks an outstanding selection of local and international publications for hobbyists, collectors and the design-savvy. Here, you'll find everything from niche surf magazines to obscure fashion titles; from leading publications such as Monocle, Wallpaper* and Vogue, to small independent titles like Deriva Paper and Four & Sons. It also offers a neat selection of books, music and DVDs. After shopping, drop by the excellent Drop Coffee at Wollmar Yxkullsgatan 10, an award-winning roastery and café.

🕐 1100-1830 (M-F), -1700 (Sa), 1200-1600 (Su)
🏠 Krukmakargatan 24-26, 118 51
📞 +46 (0)8 133 574
🔗 www.papercutshop.se

"This is the best place for magazines and it neighbours a few excellent fashion stores."

– Carl Kleiner

30 Peow! Studio
Map N, P.110

Tucked away in a quiet residential street, Peow!
Studio is a comic book publishing company
and riso print studio run by three Stockholm
illustrators. With walls lined with brightly
coloured handmade comics and zines, totes
adorned with the Peow! logo, and numerous
other collectibles, this small shop is a like a
candy store for comic book enthusiasts, and
indeed anyone with an appreciation for DIY
culture. Pick up a little something and support
this creative enterprise.

🕙 1000–1800 (M–F)
🏠 Bäckvägen 42, 126 47
📞 +46 (0)73 539 2280
URL www.peowstudio.com

*"Peow! has some of the most unique comics in town,
all printed at the spot by the artists who run the shop.
Check their hours before visiting or call Patrick Crotty."*

– Rui Tenreiro

31 Södermalms Akvarieaffär
Map I, P.109

Södermalms Akvarieaffär is home to an impressive selection of aquarium fish tanks, exotic fish and accessories. Stocked with all the equipment you could possibly require to keep your own tropical fish, the owner is especially knowledgeable on the subject and has been known to keep customers enthralled in conversation for hours. An alternative and delightful way to spend an afternoon in Stockholm.

🕐 1500–2200 (Tu), –1900 (W–F), 1200–1600 (Sa–Su)
🏠 Krukmakargatan 3, 118 51   📞 +46 (0)8 441 0180
🔗 www.sodermalmsakvarieaffar.se

"This basement is a geek's paradise, at least if your specialty is fish. Go on a Tuesday before you hit the bars and have conversations that last you the whole night."

– Björn Atldax, Vår & Cheap Monday

32 **Brandstationen**
Map I, P.109

Since 2005 Herr Judit, Stockholm's favourite vintage clothing store, has sought to champion high-quality products sourced from all over the world. Their interior store Brandstationen focuses on vintage furnishings and antiques, artfully curated for trendy and style-conscious vintage connoisseurs. Huge windows flood the store with natural light, creating a calm and relaxing atmosphere for customers to browse their growing collection of decorative objects and trinkets. Definitely a modern day treasure trove of inspiring interior items infused with history.

🕐 1100–1800 (M–F), –1700 (Sa), 1200–1600 (Su) 📍 Hornsgatan 64, 118 51
📞 +46 (0)8 658 3010
URL www.herrjudit.se/brandstationen

"There are two more vintage stores from the same owner up the street. Hornsgatan 65 and 75 – these focus more on clothing."

– Per Emanuelsson, Humans since 1982

33 Humana Second Hand
Map I, P.109

Stockholm's leading thrift and vintage store Humana Sweden offers a huge variety of clothing, shoes and accessories at knockdown prices. The sprawling store caters to both women and men, attracting a mostly young crowd. Humana Sweden is part of the international network of Humana People to People, which consists of 31 independent organisations worldwide working to create an equitable and sustainable society. Help yourself to their wide selection of secondhand goodies, while at the same time making the world a better place.

🕐 1000–1800 (M–F), 1100–1700 (Sa), 1200–1600 (Su)
🏠 Timmermansgatan 23, 118 55
☎ +46 (0)8 640 4323
URL humanasecondhand.com

"A really great vintage clothing store. Well organised and has a great selection of clothes in great condition. And it's cheap!"
– Viktor Khan

34 Epok Antik & Kuriosa
Map A, P.104

This tiny shop is filled to the brim with beautiful vintage and antique clothes, wedding dresses, veils, wax flower crowns and jewellery.
The lady who owns the shop is absolutely charming, with a broad knowledge of vintage styles. Visit Epok for a lovely vintage shopping experience and a nostalgic trip back in time. Afterwards, have a cup of coffee at the equally beautiful and retro Konditori Ritorno, which is just a few steps away. Or take a walk around the idyllic Vasaparken, one of Stockholm's most loved parks.

🕐 1100–1800 (M–F), –1600 (Sa)
🏠 Odengatan 83, 113 22   📞 +46 (0)8 341 340

> "Book ahead if you are looking for a wedding dress. Then you get access to the room upstairs that is like an attic of vintage wedding bonanza."
>
> – Linnea Olsson

35 Antikt Gammalt & Nytt
Map D, P.106

With famously grumpy owners, Antikt Gammalt & Nytt (which translates to 'Antiques Old and New') is the place to go for rare vintage accessories. The shop was opened by Tore and Mats Grundström when they discovered a warehouse-full of long-forgotten 1940s jewellery. A popular spot for stylists and dedicated followers of fashion, be prepared to jostle for the best pieces. To complete your vintage experience, have a cup of coffee at nearby Konditori Sturekatten, a quaint café located in a 17th century house with interiors resembling your fancy grandma's living room.

🕐 1100–1800 (M–F), 1200–1600 (Sa)
🏠 Mäster Samuelsgatan 11, 111 44
📞 +46 (0)8 678 3530

"Whatever you do, don't go there with a rucksack on your back. The place is small and I can promise you that you don't want to knock something over."

– Erik Bergqvist, Acne Advertising

36 Chez Albert
Map A, P.105

A cornucopia of gastronomic delights awaits you at this family-owned delicatessen. Since 1975, Chez Albert has been one of Stockholm's best-kept secrets, offering locals delectable specialties such as fine wines, traditional French cheeses, cured meats and locally sourced produce, among many others. Laden from floor to ceiling with assorted bottles, mysterious jars and colourful labels piled high onto the shelves, the store is a joy to explore. Take note of the blackboard fixed outside where daily specials are noted, alongside an attractive window display tempting hungry pedestrians.

🕐 1000–1800 (Tu–F), –1400 (Sa)
🏠 Roslagsgatan 33, 113 54
📞 +46 (0)8 612 9995
URL www.chezalbert.nu

"Ask for their homemade chorizo, remove the skin and crumble the meat in a pan. Add salt and pepper, and fry it with peeled canned tomatoes. Mix and serve with spaghetti. You're welcome."

– Tony Cederteg, Libraryman

Restaurants & Cafés

Cosy cafés, fancy meatballs and fresh organic cuisine

Stockholm is known for its wealth of independent cafés and charming *fika* culture. 'Fika' essentially means to have coffee and something small on the side – be it a cinnamon bun, a piece of cake or a *semla*. It can happen at any moment of the day, whether with family, friends or a special someone. Meanwhile, Swedish food culture is largely based on great access to local, fresh ingredients provided by a wealth of farmlands, forests, rivers and lakes. Swedes love picking herbs, berries and mushrooms in the wild – a favourite national pastime alongside fika. Besides organic restaurants, Stockholm is also dotted with modern pizza parlours, Thai kiosks, hamburger places and popular hotdog stands. Start the day with a morning *fika* at Mellqvist Kaffebar (#45), a favourite hangout of Swedish pop musicians. For lunch, go to crowd-favourite Lilla Aarts (#46) for their organic lunch time specials, or try Hermans' vegetarian lunch buffet (*Fjällgatan 23B, 116 28*). Their terrace has a stunning view of Lake Mälaren and the city skyline. For a quick lunch, you can't go wrong with a delicious specialty hotdog from street food vendor Günter's Korvar (#48). Time for fika number two? Step inside Valand (#44) and watch as time stands still, or drop by award-winning Drop Coffee (*Wollmar Yxkullsgatan 10, 118 50*) and admire their purist coffee preparation. For a working afternoon, Café Coffice (*Tjärhovsgatan 5, 116 21*) has a friendly staff and lots of working spaces, including two meeting rooms for rent. As the evening draws in, why not try traditional Swedish meatballs at the wood-panelled grand hall in Pelikan (#40), or sample the smoke-infused cuisine at hip hangout Ekstedt (#38)? For fine dining with an affordable price tag, Oaxen Slip (#42) offers a star dining experience by the harbour.

Fredrik Wetterholm
Cofounder, Another Agency

Me and my partners run Another Agency, for brands that want to digitalise their business. I was born and raised in a Stockholm suburb and now live in the city with my wife and daughter.

Nybrogatan 38
P.072

Ekstedt
P.073

Sebastian Westin
Cofounder, Sandqvist

I'm one of three founders of Sandqvist bags and items. I work as a PR and marketing manager. I love outdoor activities, fly fishing, motorcycles and golf.

Catrin Vagnemark
Co-owner, BVD

Catrin Vagnemark is one of the first women to found and lead a design bureau in Sweden and is still one of the leading creative directors in the business. BVD's philosophy is 'Simplify to Clarify'.

Ett Hem
P.074

Martin Nicolausson
Illustrator & graphic designer

Martin Nicolausson is perhaps the only Swedish illustrator and graphic designer with the name Martin Nicolausson.

Pelikan
P.076

Restaurang Indian Inn
P.077

Johan Bring
Film director & photographer

I'm a swedish film director, photographer, screenwriter, gallery owner and musician. I've lived in Stockholm since 1994.

Byggstudio
Graphic design group

Byggstudio is Hanna Nilsson and Sofia Østerhus who work mostly with interiors and public space. Nilsson has resided in Stockholm since 2008 and Østerhus in Oslo where she is originally from.

Oaxen Slip
P.078

Maja Gunn
Artist, designer & writer

My research studies fashion design methodology and I design costume for films and theatre. My tips are related to summer, as that's when I love Stockholm the most.

Salong 2
P.080

Valand Kafé Konditori
P.081

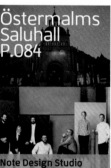

Hannah Waldron
Artist & designer

To me, weaving is a natural process to compliment my grid based images. I'm currently a research student in Craft at Konstfack, investigating how weaving tells stories.

Teenage Engineering
Product design studio

Teenage Engineering is a studio for future commercial products and communication. We create high quality, well designed, electronic products for all people who love sound and music.

Mellqvist Kaffebar
P.082

Ester Ideskog aka Vanbot
Artist & songwriter

I moved to Stockholm right after high school and have been in love with this city ever since. I perform as Vanbot and I do electronic pop music. I'm a melody junkie!

Lilla Aarts
P.083

Östermalms Saluhall
P.084

Note Design Studio
Multidisciplinary design studio

Note works within within the fields of architecture, interior, product and graphic design. Our philosophy is to stand out from the crowd: "To note something, to get noticed."

Marcus Lundin
Director

I'm a commercial and music video director. I was born in a small town in the northern parts of Sweden, and now live in Stockholm with my wife Caroline and one year old son Kid.

Günter's Korvar
P.085

37 Nybrogatan 38
Map D, P.106

Nybrogatan 38 is an extremely popular neighborhood restaurant that serves traditional Swedish dishes and old classics with a contemporary twist. Open from early morning to midnight everyday, you can enjoy a delicious breakfast, lunch or (very late) dinner here for reasonable prices. During the summer, opt for a table on their large and sunny terrace. Ask for Jonas at the bar and watch as he makes a couple of the most amazing cocktails you'll ever have.

🕑 0730–0000 (M–Tu), –0100 (W–F),
1000– (Sa), –0000 (Sun)
🏠 Nybrogatan 38, 114 40
📞 +46 (0)8 662 3322
URL www.nybrogatan38.com

"Stockholm's best choice for breakfast, brunch, lunch or dinner. You may catch me and my friends spinning records in their bar on a Friday or Saturday."

– Fredrik Wetterholm, Another Agency

38 Ekstedt

Map D, P.106

Restaurant Ekstedt was conceived from the bold idea of creating a cuisine which uses no electricity at all, only flames. Everything is cooked over an open fire (with wood sourced from Scandinavian apple trees), infusing each dish with a slightly smoky flavour. Order the baked langoustine with seaweed and pulses, or smoked beef tartare with morels, ox marrow and spring herbs, and enjoy a lavish meal at one of Stockholm's hippest hangouts.

🕑 1800 till late (Tu-Th), 1700- (F), 1600- (Sa)
🏠 Humlegårdsgatan 17, 114 46
📞 +46 (0)8 611 1210 🌐 ekstedt.nu

"This is the opposite of molecular and futuristic gastronomy. Make sure to book in advance, preferably at least three weeks ahead."

– Sebastian Westin, Sandqvist

39 Ett Hem
Map A, P.105

Ett Hem is a luxurious, red-brick boutique hotel with a low-key yet elegant ambience. Offering 12 stylish rooms, the hotel's interiors presents a sophisticated blend of contemporary and vintage design. There's also a library and a couple of sitting rooms furnished with mid-century modern décor. When it's time to dine, guests can eat and drink where they please, with choices including a walled garden, a sunny conservatory or the kitchen with its striking design features and long oak table. The atmosphere is decidedly intimate, making it an ideal destination for those looking to experience an alternative hotel stay.

🕐 *Morning till late evening daily*
🏠 *Sköldungagatan 2, 114 27*
📞 *+46 (0)8 200 590* **URL** *www.etthem.se*
📎 *Reservation required for external guests*

"An exclusive hotel with a fantastic restaurant."
– Catrin Vagnemark, BVD

40 Pelikan

Map E, P.107

Housed in a former beer hall in Södermalm, Pelikan serves up authentic Swedish home fare in a grand wood-panelled hall with high ceilings and old-world charm. Packed to the rafters by early evening, the atmosphere is relaxed and lively, as diners take full advantage of their craft beer menu while waiting for their food (which can sometimes take a while). Try their *Grosshandlarvillan* Dinner – a boiled knuckle of pork with mashed turnips and three kinds of mustard, or opt for a traditional dish of Swedish meatballs for a hearty meal. For those looking for a livelier mix of people, the sister bar Kristallen is right next door.

🕐 1600-0000 (M-Tu), -0100 (W-Th), 1200-(F- Su)
🏠 Blekingegatan 40, 116 62 📞 +46 (0)8 556 090 90
URL www.pelikan.se

"Don't be discouraged by some of the staff's lack of manners. It's part of the experience. Have SOS ('Sill och Snaps' or, herring and snaps) and meatballs."
– Martin Nicolausson

41 Restaurang Indian Inn
Map G, P.108

Having undergone something of a revival in recent years, the Hornstull district in Söder-malm has become a thriving cultural haven where many eateries, bars and food shops have taken residence. For true authentic Indian food, look no further than Indian Inn, which of-fers an eclectic menu using fresh ingredients and traditional spices. Enjoy their service and handmade furnishings as much as their nosh. Sit outside in the summer, then take a walk down to Hornstull Strand and Tanto park after your meal.

🕐 1100–2300 (M–F), 1300– (Sa–Su)
🏠 Verkstadsgatan 11–13, 117 36
📞 +46 (0)8 668 9233
URL www.indianinn.se

"Me and David have been eating here for years while planning music videos and films. Perfect Indian food and at a very nice price."

– Johan Bring

42 Oaxen Slip
Map B, P.105

Make a little escape to Oaxen, a celebrated gastronomic destination on Djurgården established by chef Magnus Ek and his wife, Agneta Green in 2013. "Slip" is the casual half of the restaurant, serving up their own interpretation of Swedish bistro fare with unique ingredients sourced from the island and the Nordic region. Weekly specials such as crayfish and grilled pork liven up the menu during the summer season. Next to Slip is"Krog", a rare fine dining gem in Stockholm with two Michelin stars. Oaxen Slip only have 10 drop-in seats at the bar for walk-in guests, so be sure you book ahead.

🕐 1700–2300 (M), 1200– (Tu–Su)
🏠 Beckholmsvägen 26, 115 21
📞 +46 (0)8 551 531 05 URL oaxen.com
📎 Kitchen takes an hour break at 4pm

"Take the boat from Slussen, then walk past the amusement park, lush greenery and old houses to the harbour – getting there is half the joy."

– Hanna Nilsson & Sofia Østerhus, Byggstudio

43 Salong 2
Map G, P.108

Salong 2 is a quaint restaurant and bar situated beside a charming little movie theatre, Bio Rio. A favourite among locals, Salong 2 offers lovely vegetarian and French-inspired cuisine, unique Swedish beers and organic wines, all served in a beautiful interior setting designed by Kristoffer Sundin and Pål Rodenius. The surroundings outside are a sight to behold as well: enjoy a stroll by the beautiful waterside, or have an after-lunch cup of coffee at nearby café Vurma.

🕐 1000–2100 daily
🏠 Hornstulls Strand 3, 117 39
🌐 www.biorio.se

"Watch a movie at the cinema Bio Rio next door."
– Maja Gunn

 **44** **Valand Kafé Konditori**
Map A, P.104

Owned by a pleasant German lady Magdalena Åström, the café was designed by her Swedish husband Stellan Åström in 1954. Decorated with original mid-century modern furniture and floor-to-ceiling teak, Valand has a timeless, classic movie appeal that is sure to leave a lasting impression. It is frequented by designers, artists and actors who enjoy the nostalgic atmosphere and the almost-sacred peace and quiet of the place. Order a freshly brewed cup of coffee, a slice of homemade *äppelkaka* (apple pie) with vanilla cream, and watch the world go by.

 Opening hours vary daily
Surbrunnsgatan 48, 113 48
+46 (0)8 300 476
Valand – Kafé Konditori

"*Beautiful atmospheric interior that hasn't changed since the fifties.*"

– Hannah Waldron

45 Mellqvist Kaffebar
Map I, P.109

A hip coffee bar with a fantastic coffee selection and traditional Swedish snacks, Mellqvist Kaffebar has a typical Söder vibe. Their charming outdoor area on a little town square is an attractive spot for people watching, whilst the interior is furnished with long high tables for students and freelancers to work in relative peace. It's also a favourite café of a few famous Swedish pop musicians. A nook at the rear of the café features several rows of reclaimed cinema seats, introducing an element of fun with your mid-morning coffee.

🕐 0700–1800 (M–F), 0900– (Sa–Su)
🏠 Hornsgatan 78, 118 21
📞 +46 (0)76 875 2992   ✦ Mellqvist Kaffebar

"Coffee, food, art and more. You can even buy our Pocket Operator synths there. Look out for celebrities going into the INGRD studio located behind."

–Teenage Engineering

46 Lilla Aarts

Map A, P.104

Passionate foodies Johanna Odebrant and Justus Aarts opened this "Little" café in 2014 following the sale of their rather more upmarket restaurant establishment *Aarts Mat och Dryck* (Aarts Food and Drink). Focusing on simple, wholesome food using local and organic ingredients, their menu changes daily, offering just a small selection of carefully prepared dishes. The colourful interior makes it a hit with the young crowd and an ideal spot for a working lunch or relaxing afternoon with a newspaper. Check out their facebook page for the current lunchtime blackboard specials, as popular dishes sell out fast.

🕐 0800-1500 (M-F)
🏠 Norrtullsgatan 24, 113 45   📞 +46 (0)8 330 400
🔳 www.aartsmat.se/aarts

> *"Come in time or call ahead to book a late lunch. Have a chat with the staff and let them tell you about the food. You'll have a hard time making them stop."*
>
> – Ester Ideskog aka Vanbot

083

47 Östermalms Saluhall
Map D, P.106

The Östermalms Saluhall is a covered market hall built at the end of the 19th century. Housed in a red-brick structure with an iron frame and roof designed by prominent Swedish architect Kasper Salin, this magnificent 'temple of food' has some 20 delicatessen stalls all decorated with carved wood. Offering a wide assortment of cheese, sausages, game and other delicacies, it is famous for high quality ingredients and cooked dishes from Swedish and international cuisine. In the summer, the square in front of the building hosts a flower, fruit and vegetable market.

🕐 0930-1800 (M-Th), -1900 (F), -1600 (Sa)
🏠 Östermalmstorg, 114 42
URL www.ostermalmshallen.se/en

"*You will find the best of Scandinavian food in this historical building.*"

– Note Design Studio

48 Günter's Korvar
Map A, P.104

Günter's Korvar offers the arguably finest sausages in town. A cross between a French hot dog and a panino, their 'bun' is a hollowed-out half-baguette that is grilled on a press and stuffed to bursting with sausage and sauerkraut. Their extensive menu offers plenty of choices. It's wise to have a back up as favourites sell out quick. Try Günters' homemade chili sauce if you're feeling brave, and enjoy your korvar in the sunshine.

🕐 1100–2000 (M–F), –1600 (Sa)
🏠 Karlbergsvägen 66, 113 35
📘 Günter's korvar
🔗 Cash only

"This is where the locals queue up for the best sausages money can buy. The line might be long but Günter's homemade chimichurri will make up for the wait."

– Marcus Lundin

Nightlife

Excellent live music, parties under a bridge and magical nightswimming

The Swedish capital has really come to life as a party city of international standards. Nothing proves this better than the many open-air sessions that go on in and around the city on boats, in forests and under bridges from dusk 'till dawn. Don't let the reserved and shy exterior of the Swedes fool you. When the alcohol is flowing, their true fun-loving nature comes out and you better be ready for the night of your life. The evening starts with a *förfest* (pre-party), as revellers gather in friends' living rooms with their Systembolaget-bought drinks. Alcohol is expensive in Sweden, especially at bars, so locals try to maximise the night by already drinking at home with their less expensive stock from the government-regulated store, before heading out to the pricier clubs. If you feel like a king, kick off the night with cocktails at fancy French bar Riche (#54) or Hawaiian-themed Tiki Room (#53). Then, ease yourself into the evening's entertainment at hip lounge bar Slakthuset (#51), and take in a gorgeous sunset at one of its many rooftop parties. Check out the gigs at Debaser Medis or Strand (#50), which are excellent venues for live music and touring acts. For a truly unforgettable experience, go to Trädgården (#49) which offers an awe-inspiring mix of dance floors, street food and game areas nestled under a towering concrete bridge. Play ping pong, dance, meet new friends, and say yes when they invite you to the after-party. To seal the magical night, take a dip in one of the city's many lakes. Långholmen (#60) is a good spot, but you can jump in anywhere actually. Float on your back and bask under the surrealistic midnight sun. There's nothing like it in the world.

Jonas Wagell
Architect & designer

My studio is in Hornstull, but recent projects reach as far as Asia and North America. Our work with products and architecture has been recognised as simplistic playfulness and clever compact living.

Debaser Strand
P.092

Lina Forsgren
Graphic designer & art director

I'm a freelance graphic designer at Reform Act and I co-run Feministiska kommunikationsbyrån. I work across disciplines within different fields.

Cho Hyunjung
Founder, J0o0lry

Evident in the name, J0o0lry's mission is to explore within the scope of body related artefact using unreadable language. J0o0lry launched its first commercial project in 2014.

Trädgården
P.090

Slakthuset
P.093

Karl Grandin
Cofounder, Vår & Cheap Monday

After art directing for Swedish music magazine *Pop*, I set up Vår and Cheap Monday with Björn Atldax. Today I freelance and do art projects, encompassing all things from drawings to alchemy.

Tiki Room
P.095

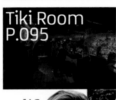

Clara Nordlander Wiberg
Cofounder, Francis Floor

I'm a creative director and a Swedish champion in both artistic gymnastics and team gymnastics. My dad is my biggest inspiration. My life goal is to visit all countries in the world.

TWENTY-FIVE
25 AH
ART HOUSE

25AH
Brand & design agency

25AH is founded by three friends from Forsbergs School of Design. Among our assignments you will find strategic visual communication for advertising, branding and exhibitions.

Mbargo
P.094

Riche
P.096

Brendan Austin
Photographer

Through fictional landscapes, I question how we perceive both the reality of the image and how we experience the world around us. I currently live in Stockholm with my wife and two sons.

Fredrik Lund-Hansen
Cofounder, Rebels Studios

Parallel to my creative studio, Rebels Studios, I run skateboard company, Up South, together with my friend Douglas Bielke. I used to live in New York but now I'm back in Stockholm again.

Agneta Green
Owner, Oaxen Krog & Slip

I live and work with my husband Magnus Ek on Djurgården where we run our restaurants. When I am off work I go on long walks with our dog, named Ringo Star, as he's born on the day we got our first Michelin star.

Anna Giertz
Illustrator & musician

Originally from Gotland, I have been living in Stockholm for years where I work as an illustrator and musician.

Jonas Jacob Svensson
Photographer

My work falls within the fields of documentary and editorial photography, with a focus on portraits. I produce images for magazines and advertising. I'm based in Stockholm but work wherever necessary.

Quiltland
Musician

I'm a musician and a pattern cutter living in Stockholm.

49 Trädgården
Map E, P.107

Trädgården (Tree Garden) is an outdoor wonderland which includes a bar, lounge, club and concert venue, located under a huge bridge in Skanstull. This one-of-a-kind venue is where the hipster youth of Stockholm gather throughout the summer for ping-pong, *boule*, retro video game consoles or for partying 'till dawn. They also have live acts and an art gallery on site. In the colder months of October to April, Trädgården magically turns into Under Bron (Under the Bridge). Both are definitely the cool crowd's favourite hangout places, all year-round.

⊙ ⑤ Opening hours & admission vary with events
🏠 Hammarby Slussväg 2, 118 60
URL www.tradgarden.com, www.husetunderbron.se

"Check website for free concerts. Turn up early to avoid standing in line for hours, which unfortunately is mandatory after 11 pm most days during the summer."
– Jonas Wagell

50 Debaser Strand
Map G, P.108

Tucked away in a basement, hidden on the waterside of Hornstull Strand lies the grungy intimate concert hall known as Debaser Strand. Strand has become a bit of a cult favorite amongst Stockholm's music lovers with its dark, edgy and intimate atmosphere, small stage and limited seating areas. The bar has an industrial feel to it that fits in just right with the rest of the pared down interior. Performances range from established names to up-and-coming live acts. Expect a warm, buzzing atmosphere, decent sound system and a mixed crowd.

🕐 💲 *Bar Brooklyn: 1800–0100 (W–Th), –0300 (F–Sa), showtime & admission vary with programmes*
🏠 *Hornstulls Strand 4, 117 39* ☎ *+46 (0)8 658 6350*
🔗 *debaser.se*

"*My favourites are the feminist club nights. In the summer, you can bring your own beer and sit outside on the small pier before you enter the club.*"

– Lina Forsgren

 Slakthuset
Map C, P.105

Slakthuset is a popular lounge bar and nightclub with a creative and artsy vibe, often frequented by the stylish and fashionable crowds. Located in the industrial district of Johanneshov close to the Ericsson Globe (#4), the 1000-capacity venue offers an eclectic lineup of DJs playing a mix of house, deep bass, techno, underground and hip-hop. Open all year round, their outdoor rooftop parties are especially popular, featuring special guest performances that will keep you moving from sunset 'till sunrise.

🕐 1700–0300 (F–Sa)
🏠 Slakthusgatan 6, 121 62
f Slakthuset

"Like most of the other clubs in Stockholm, things get more interesting after midnight. Check out their facebook page for details on the night's event."

– Cho Hyunjung, J0o0lry

 Mbargo
Map G, P.108

Located in the hip Hornstull area next to Austrian restaurant Moldau, this laid-back, intimate bar offers a great selections of reasonably priced beers. Choices feature a range of Swedish and Danish microbrews, including familiar names like Omnipollo, Mikkeller and Dugges Ale & Porterbryggeri. With an eclectic decor and a mixed clientele, Mbargo is a rare gem in a sea of fancy, overpriced bars in the city. Grab a drink and feel welcome.

🕐 1800–0100 (M–Sa), –2200 (Su)
🏠 Bergsunds Strand 37, 117 38

"Perfect for beers before or after dinner at restaurant Barbro or Cantina Real, seeing a gig at Debaser Strand or having drinks at Calexico or Tjoget, all close by."

– Karl Grandin, Vår & Cheap Monday

53 Tiki Room
Map A, P.104

One floor down and suddenly you'll find yourself in Hawaii. Or at least what we think Hawaii
would look like: warm, sweaty and everyone
wearing Hawaiian shirts. Tiki Room's interior
has blowfishes on the ceiling, tribal masks on
the wall, and even a TV on the bar with 70s
surf films on repeat. The quirky bar offers killer
cocktails and dancing 'till late. Music veers on
the loud side, so if you're looking to make conversation with your friends, the much quieter
Mellow Bar (located upstairs) is probably more
to your taste.

🕐 1700-0100 (M-Th, Sa), 1600- (F)
🏠 Birkgaten 10, 113 36 📞 +46 (0)8 331 555
📘 Tiki Room

"Be aware of the Volcano drink. It tastes like heaven
but will give you hell! Sometimes that's good, and
sometimes that's bad."

– Clara Nordlander Wiberg

54 Riche
Map D, P.106

Founded in 1893, Riche strove to imitate its Parisian model, Café Riche on Boulevard des Italiens, in its interior decoration as well as in character. Starched linen tablecloths, elegant gold-framed mirrors and crystal chandeliers make for a classic yet intimate venue in the heart of town. A popular spot to start the night before hitting Stockholm's many clubs, weekends at Riche can be loud and crowded but generally upbeat and lively. Check out the notoriously fun toilet surveillance art by Jonas Dahlberg, and the exquisite rug on the wall by Märta Måås-Fjetterström, one of Sweden's most prominent textile artists.

🕙 1100–0000 (Su–M), –0200 (Tu–Sa)
🏠 Birger Jarlsgatan 4, 114 34
📞 +46 (0)8 545 035 60   URL riche.se

"Stay all night or start your evening here before heading off to the many clubs and bars around Riche. Check out the art in Lilla Baren (Little Bar) next door."
– 25AH

55 Bleck

Map E, P.107

Injecting a bit of life into the quieter parts of Södermalm, restaurant Bleck offers a relaxed dining experience in the lush and leafy setting of Lilla Blecktornsparken (Little Park). Quickly becoming a firm favourite amongst locals, the restaurant, designed by architect Johan Lytz, serves a fine selection of gastro-inspired dishes complemented by an extensive beer and cocktail menu. The friendly staff, attractive surroundings and affordability are the qualities that bring people back time and time again. Bleck operates a strict no-reservation policy, so just show up and be surprised.

🕐 1700–2300 (Su–W), –0100 (Th–Sa), brunch: 1200–1530 (Sa–Su) 🏠 Katarina Bangata 68, 116 42
📞 +46 (0)70 555 6456 🌐 restaurangbleck.se

"This place is best in the summer. Arrive early for a beer or wine on the courtyard overlooking the park."

– Brendan Austin

56 Häktet
Map I, P.109

Häktet Vänster is a tiny hidden cocktail bar in Södermalm, serving up some of the city's best drinks. Häktet means 'jail' in Swedish, as this place was actually a prison back in 1781. Shrouded in an air of mystery, you have to ring the bell before entering; when you're buzzed in, you climb up the stairs to enter the prohibition-era bar. Locals come here to kick off their weekend with trendy cocktails, such as the Luchador Belt and the Chocolate Sensual. The bar is quite popular, so consider yourself lucky if you get in.

🕐 1700–0000 (M–Tu), –0100 (W), –0300 (Th–Sa), wine bar: 1800– (Th–Sa) 🏠 Hornsgatan 82, 118 21
📞 +46 (0)8 845 910 URL haktet.se

"On arrival, try to push the door on your left. If it's locked, it means the place is full. Otherwise, walk in and have a drink at this bar within a bar."

– Fredrik Lund-Hansen, Rebels Studios

57 Babette

Map A, P.105

A tiny restaurant and bar located in an area called 'Siberia', Babette offers a menu and wine list that changes every day. Standard composition contains pizzas and snacks, five to seven starters, two main courses, cheese and dessert. The excellent selection of wine, combined with a warm and friendly atmosphere, make for a cosy and relaxing evening out. If you fancy eating somewhere else before getting drinks here, Sibiriens Soppkök on the same street is a family-run kitchen specialising in soup.

🕐 1700 till late daily   🏠 Roslagsgatan 6, 113 55
📞 +46 (0)8 509 022 24   URL babette.se

"*Magnus and I don't go out so much, but the staff often go here after we close. Each wine is purchased in small quantities and most run out the same evening.*"

– Agneta Green, Oaxen Krog & Slip

 58 Omnipollos Hatt
Map E, P.107

Rustic pilsners, new school pizzas and home-made pickles – the list spells out the magical gastronomic experience that awaits guests in Omnipollos Hatt. Jointly brought by Swedish nomadic brewery Omnipollo and local pizzeria Pizzahatt, this earthly watering hole has its floor, lamp and tiles specially done by local artists whilst Cheap Monday and the brewery's co-founder Karl Grandin spruces up their beer bottles to match their impeccable beers. While you're there, patiently wait for your light and fluffy sourdough pizzas to come out from their rather comedic woodfire pizza oven. Try as many beer as you can, as many are exclusively served here.

🕐 1200–0100 daily   🏠 Hökens Gata 3, 116 46
🔳 www.omnipolloshatt.com
f Omnipollos hatt

 "Check the bathroom. There are plenty of delicate details to look at."
– Anna Giertz

59 Night Camping

For those with a taste for adventure, Sweden's *Allemansrätt* (Right of Public Access) is a unique institution in Sweden, allowing everyone the freedom to roam the stunning Swedish countryside on land and water – providing visitors do so respectfully. You can swim or sail almost anywhere, take scenic walks or find a quiet place to sit in the national parks and nature reserves, climb a mountain or moor up on a tiny island in the archipelago. Visit one of the many camp sites such as the southwest suburb Bredäng, or go for a truly wild camping experience and pitch a tent for a night or two in a far-away, secluded spot.

URL www.naturvardsverket.se

"I promise you will find nothing alike in the city centre. So take advantage of the right of public access: tack your tent and go out in the woods."

– Jonas Jacob Svensson

60 Nightswimming at Långholmen

Map G, P.108

Steal a moment away from the endless parties on offer in central Stockholm to experience the peaceful tranquillity of Långholmen Island. A popular spot for picnics, walks and swimming, Långholmen is often described as a green oasis in the city. Float away in Lake Mälaren on a night swim during the summer months, and enjoy the surrealistic charm that this spot has to offer. Combined with the stunning beauty of the midnight sun, nightswimming memories in Stockholm is something that will stay in your heart for a long, long time.

URL langholmen.com

"Here you can take off your clothes and let your makeup float away in the Mälaren. Don't forget to take in the view of the City Hall across the water."

– Quiltland

DISTRICT MAP : **VASASTAN, VASASTADEN**

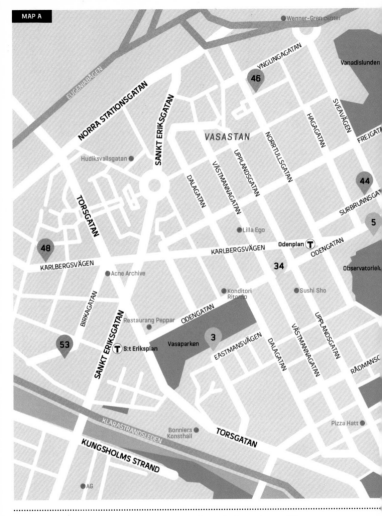

MAP A

- 3_Sven-Harrys Konst-museum
- 5_Stockholms Stadsbibliotek
- 34_Epok Antik & Kuriosa
- 44_Valand Kafé Konditori
- 46_Lilla Aarts
- 48_Günter's Korvar
- 53_Tiki Room

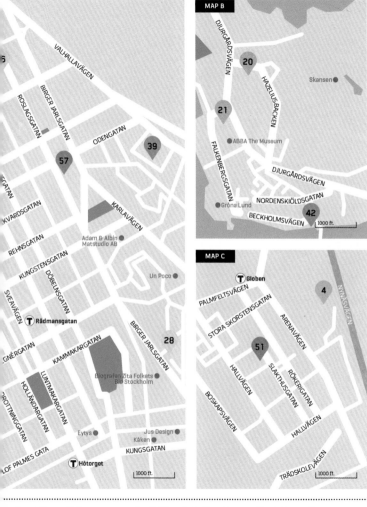

- 4_Ericsson Globe
- 20_Biologiska Museet
- 21_Liljevalchs
- 28_Rönnells Antikvariat
- 36_Chez Albert
- 39_Ett Hem
- 42_Oaxen Slip
- 51_Slakthuset
- 57_Babette

DISTRICT MAP : NORRMALM, ÖSTERMALM, GAMLA STAN, SKEPPSHOLMEN

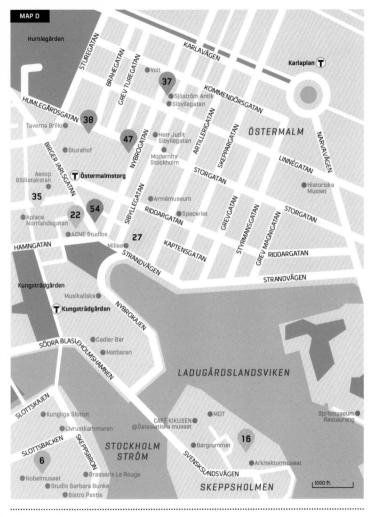

MAP D

- 6_Gamla Stan
- 16_Moderna Museet
- 22_Hallwylska Museet
- 27_Svenskt Tenn
- 35_Antikt Gammalt & Nytt
- 37_Nybrogatan 38
- 38_Ekstedt
- 47_Östermalms Saluhall
- 54_Riche

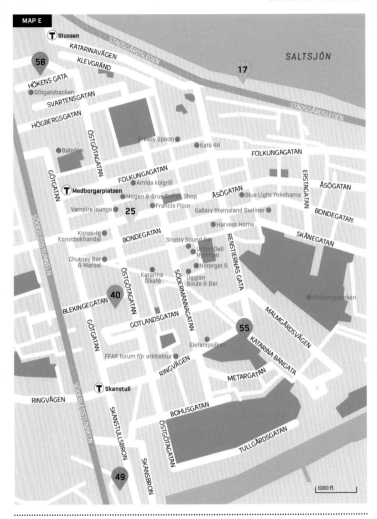

MAP E

- 17_Fotografiska
- 25_Stutterheim
- 40_Pelikan
- 49_Trädgården
- 55_Bleck
- 58_Omnipollos Hatt

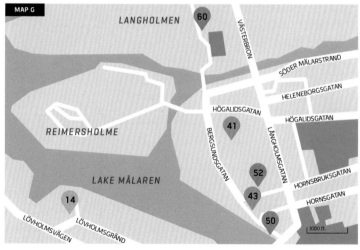

- 7_Stadshuset
- 13_Kulturhuset Stadsteatern
- 14_Färgfabriken
- 41_Restaurang Indian Inn
- 43_Salong 2
- 50_Debaser Strand
- 52_Mbargo
- 60_The cliffs of Långholmen

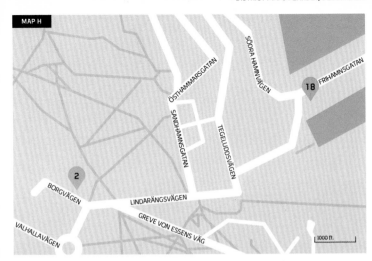

- 2_Filmhuset
- 11_Skinnarviksberget
- 18_Magasin III
- 24_Seriegalleriet
- 26_Our Legacy
- 29_Papercut
- 31_Södermalms Akvarieaffär
- 32_Brandstationen
- 33_Humana Second Hand
- 45_Mellqvist Kaffebar
- 56_Häktet

DISTRICT MAPS : **SUNDBYBERG, VÄRMDÖ, KRISTINEBERG, JOHANNESHOV, HÄGERSTEN, ENSKEDEDALEN**

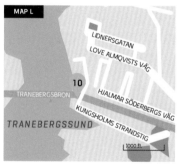

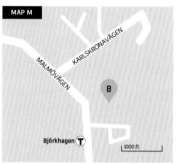

- 8_Markuskyrkan
- 9_Skogskyrkogården
- 10_Tranebergsbron
- 15_Artipelag
- 19_Marabouparken
- 23_Kulturföreningen Tellus
- 30_Peow! Studio

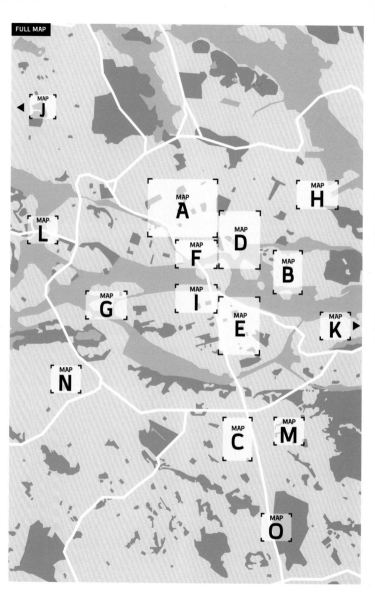

Accommodation

Hip hostels, fully-equipped apartments & swanky hotels

No journey is perfect without a good night's sleep to recharge. Whether you're backpacking or on a business trip, our picks combine top quality and convenience, whatever your budget.

($) < 800 SEK **($)** 801–1600 **($)** 1601+

Ett Hem

Ett Hem lives up to its name that translates as "A home". A former private residence built in 1910, this townhouse provides a tranquil homey space steeped in the Scandinavian aesthetics. Discerning guests will enjoy their comfortable interiors, spacious suites and a courtyard garden full of summery whiteness of light. A fully-equipped gym, a traditional Swedish sauna and and a hot stone slab will be at your disposal.

🏠 *Sköldungagatan 2, 114 27*
🕐 *+ 46 (0)8 200 590* **URL** *www.etthem.se*

HTL Kungsgatan

HTL hotels is a new four-star boutique hotel chain with modern rooms and a no-fuss approach that ensure comfortable stay at a reasonable price. Stockholm Central Station is just five minutes walk away. Its Kungsgatan location means the Royal Castle, Gamla Stan and the waterfront are all nearby.

🏠 Kungsgatan 53, 111 22
📞 +46 (0)8 410 841 50   URL htlhotels.com   💲

Miss Clara

Housed in an Art Nouveau building, originally built as the girl's school Ateneum in 1910, Miss Clara is a Swedish boutique hotel under Nobis Group. Its 92 well-designed single and double rooms and suits, all highlighted by dark herringbone parquet floors and industrial materiality. All public areas are wheelchair accessible, with rooms customised for special needs.

🏠 Sveavägen 48, 111 34   📞 +46 (0)8 440 6700
🔗 www.missclarahotel.com

Hotel J

🏠 Ellensviksvägen 1, 131 28
📞 +46 (0)8 601 3000
URL www.hotelj.com

Hotel Skeppsholmen

🏠 Gröna gången 1, Box 1616, 111 49
📞 +46 (0)8 407 2300
URL www.hotelskeppsholmen.se/en

Notes

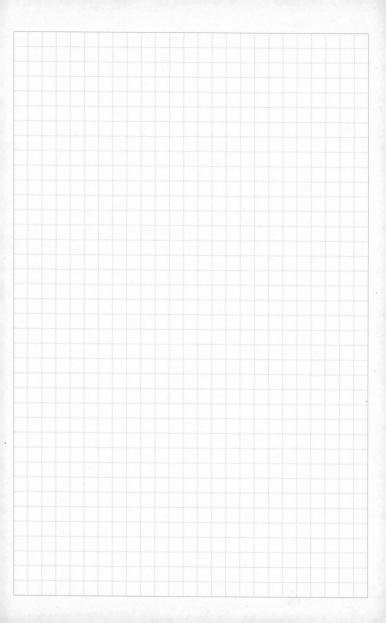

Index

Photo & other credits

In Accommodation: all courtesy
of respective hotels.

CITIX60

CITIx60: Stockholm

First published and distributed by
viction workshop ltd

viction:ary™

7C Seabright Plaza, 9-23 Shell Street,
North Point, Hong Kong

Url: www.victionary.com
Email: we@victionary.com
🅵 www.facebook.com/victionworkshop
🐦 www.twitter.com/victionary_
🅦 www.weibo.com/victionary

Edited and produced by viction:ary

Concept & art direction: Victor Cheung
Research & editorial: Queenie Ho, Caroline Kong
Project coordination: Jovan Lip, Katherine Wong
Design & map illustration: Frank Lo, MW Wong

Contributing editor: Angel Trinidad
Contributing writer: Lisa Hassell
Cover map illustration: Gustav Dejert
Count to 10 illustrations: Guillaume Kashima aka Funny Fun
Photography: Gerard Puigmal

Content is compiled based on facts available as of August 2015. Travellers are
advised to check for updates from respective locations before your visit.

First edition
· ISBN 978-988-13203-8-4
Printed and bound in China

Acknowledgements

A special thank you to all creatives, photographer(s), editor, producers, com-
panies and organisations for your crucial contributions to our inspiration and
knowledge necessary for the creation of this book. And, to the many whose
names are not credited but have participated in the completion of the book,
we thank you for your input and continuous support all along.